Twelve Choices:

Life Changing Choices You Must Make

by Wilson Adams

Published by
Spiritbuilding Publishers
9700 Ferry Road, Waynesville, OH 45068

(800) 282–4901

TWELVE CHOICES:
Life Changing Choices You Must Make
by Wilson Adams

ISBN: 978–1–7363224–9–9

All Scripture references are from the New American Standard Bible, 1960, 1962, 1963, 1968, 1971, 1975, 1977, 1995 THE LOCKMAN FOUNDATION Used by permission (*www.Lockman.org*).

Printed in the USA by D & E Printing, Brownsburg, IN   *dandeprinting.com*

Spiritbuilding
PUBLISHERS

spiritbuilding.com
Spiritual equipment for the contest of life

Table of Contents:
I Choose to ...

I Choose to Believe in God

Genesis 1:1

In the beginning God created the heavens and the earth.

C hoices. I grew up hearing the oft-repeated phrase, "God made us free moral agents." Defined, it simply meant that God made us and gave us the freedom to choose. And life—reduced to its essence—is all about the choices we make. There is no denying or escaping the personal power of choice that God gives to every human being.

I have set before you life and death, blessing and curse.
Therefore choose life (Deuteronomy 20:19).

If it is disagreeable in your sight to serve the Lord,
choose for yourselves today whom you will serve (Joshua 24:15).

Choices. The most powerful advantage God places in our hands is the power to choose. I may not be able to choose my circumstances, but I can always choose my response. **Q:** Why do some respond to tragedy better than others? **A:** Because they choose to. Make the right life-choices and other things fall into place. Make the wrong life-choices and things will go from bad to worse.

Choices. Life comes down to a series of choices for which you are both responsible and accountable. You cannot pass the buck on any of these, plead ignorance, or make excuses. And remember this: a refusal to choose is to choose. So, what choices have you made?

The most crucial decision you will ever make involves
personal faith in the Creator. Do you believe in God?

I. Lord, I Believe!

A. Some have the idea that certain ones are born with faith like they are born with blue eyes and brown hair. No. Each individual must make this life-changing choice (Jeremiah 29:13–14). It's not like God reveals His presence to some and hides Himself from others (Romans 1:20). Although God markets His existence worldwide 24/7/365 (Psalm 19:1–4), some choose to embrace the evidence while others choose to ignore it.

B. "In the beginning..." Isn't it interesting how the Bible begins? One might expect Scripture to lead off with a detailed explanation about God, His nature, and a definitive apologetic as to why you should believe in Him. It doesn't. The Bible begins with an assumption: assuming that rational people will grasp the obvious: a Supreme Being superior to man did all this! Thus, without elaboration or explanation, we are simply told: "In the beginning God..."

Imagine walking in the woods and happening upon a campsite— complete with tents, clothing on the line, and a coffee pot over a smoldering fire. No one on their right mind would conclude that such just "happened" or "evolved." Anyone with common sense would know by the evidence that someone had been there previously and created the scene. The Bible begins with the same assertion—yet adds the information that "God" is responsible.

1. Think about: (1) the delicate balance of nature, (2) the intricate construction of the human body, or (3) the marvelous precision of the solar system. Each of these demands a superior intellect with unlimited creative power. It's no wonder the psalmist declared, "The fool has said in his heart, 'There is no God.'"

2. In an amazing twist of logic, those who deny the existence of God often deride believers for "checking their brains

at the door." No, logic demands that a creation has a Creator; that a design has a Designer.

II. Christians and Inferiority Complexes.
   A. Too many believers have been intimidated by a godless world into questioning the credibility of believing in God. Peter addresses the issue in 1 Peter 3:15. He literally says that you must "set forth reasons why you believe." Someone somewhere and some place will ask you the question: Why do you believe in God? Can you answer the question intelligently? Keep in mind: Peter would not have issued the challenge to give answers for faith if there were no answers.

   • **The cosmological answer:** for every effect there must be a cause. If I work in the garden with a hoe and develop a blister on my hand—that's cause and effect. Yet science stumbles when it comes to creation—not because the argument is weak, but because to admit a universe of cause-effect is to admit a Creator. And if there is a Creator, then I must deal with the issue of personal accountability. And if there is personal accountability, I cannot choose to live any way I wish. Remember this: it's easier to profess doubt in God than to live for Him.

   • **The evidential argument:** order requires pre-thought and design. My friend, Bill, has a beautifully restored '67 Camaro (the kind of muscle-car that guys drool over). Can you imagine the looks Bill would receive if he tried to convince someone that one day he heard a *big bang*—and suddenly there it was. Who would believe that? No one. Yet every day young people are subject to the world of academia that seeks to convince them of the same kind of logic (?).

   • **The moral argument:** if there is no God, where did man get his moral compass? Could it be that the Creator gave to human beings something He did not give to the animal world: a moral code of conscience—? No one calls 9–1–1 when a dog steals a steak from a neighbor's grill. Yet, man is aware of a moral code. Where did that come from if not instilled within him by the Creator?

B. *You shall love the Lord with...all your mind* (Matthew 22:37). Christianity is an intelligent faith. God wants you to use your mind to examine the evidence and reach a conclusion.

III. Challenges to Faith—1 Corinthians 3:18–20.

A. "Useless" philosophies all have a common denominator: they seek to dethrone God and enthrone man.

- *Humanism*—a man-centered philosophy that seeks to solve man's problems by man himself.
- *Secularism*—cloaked in the "separation of church and state," this philosophy, in reality, seeks to separate man from God.
- *New Age*—is nothing more than re-cycled pantheism: God is whatever you want Him to be. As a result, people worship the creation rather than the Creator (Rom.1:25).
- *Evolution*—a cute way of making men out of monkeys and monkeys out of men. Science or science-fiction?—is certainly a legitimate question.

B. Any theory is "useless" if God is removed from the equation. Who faces the greatest dilemma: the one challenged to prove there is a God or the one challenged to prove there isn't?

C. *Everyone lives by faith.* That's true for the professor advocating the evolutionary theory as it is for the Christian who believes in God. The professor wasn't there in the beginning and neither were you. The issue has always been: what is more credible and reasonable to believe—that life came from an unknown cause and evolved over millions of years or "In the beginning God created..."

Psalm 19:1

Evidence for God is seen in the creation itself.

Psalm 139:14

Evidence for God is seen in the wonders of the human body.

1 Peter 1:24–25

Evidence for God is seen in the origin and preservation of the Bible.

John 1:1, 14

Evidence for God is seen in the Person of Jesus Christ: fulfilled prophecies, eyewitness testimony, the empty tomb, etc.

In the face of evidence, what is your choice?

Discussion Questions
Prompting Additional Insight

1. God made us free moral agents. What does that mean?

2. Why do you think some struggle with having a personal faith in God?

3. The three great questions about man have been: (1) Who am I? (2) Why am I here? (3) Where am I going?—and speak to our origin, purpose, and destiny. How do these questions relate to one's belief in God?

4. What condition does Jeremiah give in order for our search for God to be successful (29:13)?

5. The sun is 93 million miles from earth—the perfect distance to support life. Any closer and we burn up; farther away and we freeze to death. Is this merely coincidental? What argument is made in Psalm 19:1-4?

6. How do you explain that man has an inherent desire to worship? Such is seen throughout history and in every culture. Could it be that because man is a rational being, he is able to discern his surroundings and come to a common-sense conclusion: *Someone greater than man did all this!?* And does not that admission prompt you to worship? Discuss.

   Follow-up: What does Paul say in Romans 1:20 about any who would claim ignorance of God's existence?

7. Who would open a garage with thousands of dominoes standing end upon end in perfect ordered succession and exclaim, "Wow! What blew up in here?" If you said, "No one," you would be right. Yet "smart" people use that as a plausible theory to explain man's origins and surroundings. What is the psalmist's conclusion in 14:1?

8. "I'm not sure I believe in God," said a former Christian to the dismay of others. Then it came out that he was having a relationship with a woman other than his wife. Why is immorality such a convenience excuse to claim disbelief in God?

I Choose to Believe the Bible as God's Word

Psalm 19:7–11

They [words of God] are more desirable than gold...

David makes two arguments in Psalm 19: (1) God is—as evidenced by the creation (vv. 1–6) and (2) God speaks—as evidenced by the words He spoke and preserved for man (vv. 7–11). While the heavens communicate the reality and creativity of God, they cannot answer what man must do to incur divine favor. The sun may give evidence of God's power and design, but it cannot speak. You can hug a tree all day long and into the night, but it cannot tell you what the Creator wants you to do in response to Him.

Our God, however, is not silent. He has revealed His will and made it available to us. In Psalm 19:7–9, David lists six distinctive names for God's revelation, six appropriate adjectives describing His word, and six effects produced. What other book can do that? Hence, our God is alive and He has spoken (Hebrews 1:1–2).

How valuable are His words? David said they are better than gold and sweeter than honey (v. 10). Paul said, "All Scripture is inspired by God and profitable for teaching" (1 Timothy 3:16). Jesus said, "Man shall not live on bread alone, but on every word that proceeds out of the mouth of God" (Matthew 4:4). And Moses urged his people to take to heart God's words and make them your life (Deuteronomy 32:46–47). What a priceless and precious treasure you have in your Bible.

I. The Reliability of the Bible

    A. The bibliographical test. Do we have the original New Testament manuscripts? No. That's probably a good thing since man tends to turn artifacts into shrines to be worshiped. Since we don't have the originals, can the copies be trusted? Yes!

        1. Did you know that we don't have the original manuscripts of Julius Caesar, Aristotle, or Homer either? Yet those classical works of ancient literature are embraced in every university. There must be no double standard when it comes to determining authenticity.

        2. Without the originals, two things must be considered: (1) the time interval—how much time elapsed from the original to the earliest copies, and (2) the number— how many manuscripts or copies have been handed down? The more copies, the better are the opportunities for comparison and determination of accuracy.

        3. When it comes to works of antiquity, the time span is often 1000 years or more between the originals of Caesar, Aristotle, or Homer and the earliest copies. In contrast, the evidence for Scripture is amazing!

- The earliest manuscript (a small portion of John) dates to 100–150 AD—just 50–75 after the original.
- The Chester Beatty papyrus includes a major portion of the New Testament and dates to 155 AD.
- The Bodmer papyrus II is most of the gospel of John and dates to 150–200 AD.
- The three oldest books in the world (Codex Vaticanus, Codex Sinaiticus, and the Alexandrian Manuscript) contain most of the Bible and date from 325–350 AD— 250–300 years after the New Testament originals.

The force of these discoveries is to reduce the gap between the earliest manuscripts and traditional dates of the New Testament books so far that it becomes negligible in any discussion of their authenticity. No other ancient book has anything like such early and plentiful testimony to its text, and no unbiased scholar would deny that the text that has come down to us is substantially sound.

—Sir Frederick Kenyon
(former director of the British Museum).

4. And when it comes to the number of copies, there is no comparison between the Bible and other works of antiquity. For example: Caesar and the Gallic Wars—10 manuscripts. The works of Plato—7 manuscripts. Artistotle's writings—5 manuscripts. Even *The Illiad* by Homer—643 manuscripts. Compare these numbers to—

The New Testament:
5,300 Greek manuscripts and over 10,000 Latin manuscripts

5. No book comes close to the Bible when the bibliographical test for reliability is considered.

B. The internal test. Are there discrepancies that would discredit reliability? Most alleged discrepancies have long been solved by the spade of the archeologist. One key fact in substantiating the New Testament is that the writers were eyewitness or interviewed those who were (Luke 1:1–4; John 19:35; 2 Peter 1:16; 1 John 1:1–4). That meant they had to be accurate since many of their readers would have also been eyewitnesses to events described (Acts 2:22; 26:26).

C. The external text. Do other historical materials confirm or deny the Scriptures? From hundreds of early letters written by others to the findings of archeology, Scripture is confirmed time and again. Dr. Nelson Glueck (renowned Jewish archeologist) said, "No archeological discovery has ever contradicted the Scriptures."

You find an old photo of your great-grandfather that is faded, cracked, and colored. You make a copy in order to preserve it. Technically, it is not the actual photo, but it is so much like the original that you have no problem saying: "Here is a picture of my great-grandfather." It's the same with the Bible.

II. What about the Old Testament?
When you learn about the meticulous details of the Old Testament scribes, you understand why the copies are so exact. The 1948 discovery of the Dead Sea Scrolls merely confirmed their work and accuracy. *Note:* for more information on the Bible's reliability, see Josh McDowell's book—*Evidence That Demands a Verdict.*

III. The Uniqueness of the Bible.
   * *...in continuity:* written over 1,500 years by 40 different authors from different places and times and in different languages—yet telling one story!
   * *...in circulation:* printed in more languages than any other book, its circulation is unequaled. The *New York Times* stopped placing the Bible on its Best Seller Lists for good reason—with seven *billion* copies in circulation, no other book comes close.
   * *...in survival:* through time, persecution, and criticism, the Bible remains.

While its uniqueness in these areas does not prove its inspiration, it does argue that any book with these credentials is deserving of examination. The influence of the Bible is unparalleled. For example, why do Muslim countries outlaw the Bible? Could it be they know that any comparison between the Bible and the Koran would be no comparison at all?

IV. One Key Question/Answer and Three Musts.

    A. The Key *Question:* How do I know when the Word of God has become my life-authority? The Key *Answer:* When it stops you dead in your tracks! When you allow the mirror of the Word to convict your life, then you will know (Hebrews 4:12; James 1:23–25).

        1. God's word means nothing to you until you make the choice to allow it to change you. "There is a way that seems right to a man, but..." (Proverbs 14:12). When you allow the Scripture to direct your life, it doesn't seem right, it is right!

        2. "Your word is a lamp unto my feet, and a light to my path" (Psalm 119:105). Are you allowing it to show you the way?

    B. Three musts:

        1. *I must read it.* What does God want me to know?

        2. *I must embrace it,* apply what I have read, and use it to defeat the devil (Psalm 119:9; 2 Timothy 2:15).

        3. *I must recommend it to others.* The same power that will transform your life will transform the lives of your friends.

Discussion Questions
Prompting Additional Insight

1. According to Psalm 19:7–9, what effects are produced by Scripture?

2. According to 1 Thessalonians 2:13, what will the word of God accomplish?

3. What advice would you give someone to help them move from merely reading the Bible as a discipline to desiring and delighting in His word?

4. James 4:7 tells you to "resist the devil and he will flee from you." Note: we are not told to argue with him. Why not? How did Jesus defeat him in Matthew 4:1–11?

5. No one questions the copies we have of the writings of Caesar, Aristotle, Homer, etc. Yet those copies are few and far between. Contrast that to the amazing number of manuscripts available for the Bible along with the shorter time-span between the originals and the copies. In view of the strong evidence for the accuracy and authenticity of the Bible, why do you think some are hesitant to believe?

6. Use the Internet to learn about the Dead Sea Scrolls. List two or three facts about them and how they provide greater credibility for the Bible.

7. How do you think the Bible has survived through the ages in light of those who have sought to destroy it? What is the promise in 1 Peter 1:24–25?

8. Discuss the following analogies wherein some treat the Bible like:
   ...*seat-belts*—a nuisance that cramps their lifestyle
   ...*high school algebra*—technically true, but how practical is it?
   ...*a salad-bar*—where you pick and choose what you want to eat
   Then contrast those attitudes with that of the centurion in Matthew 8:5–10.

9. A GPS will take you from where you are to where you want to be. The Bible is your spiritual GPS—a roadmap from earth to heaven. Discuss what this choice has meant to your life.

I Choose to Become a Christian
Acts 16:30–34

Sirs, what must I do to be saved?

O nce a person comes to terms with the reality of the Creator (choice #1) and embraces the Bible as God's word based upon the evidence of its authenticity (choice #2), he/she then must choose whether or not they will respond to the call of the gospel.

Sin occurs when we make wrong choices and walk away from God and His revealed will. The sad result of sin: we are separated from God (Isaiah 59:1–2) and eventually everyone falls (Romans 3:23). Through God's grace in the sending of Jesus, He has provided a way of forgiveness and the promise of eternal life. In response to the question asked on the day of Pentecost in Acts 2:37, the apostle Peter responded by saying, "Repent, and each of you be baptized in the name of Jesus Christ for the forgiveness of your sins..."

Like the others, this choice is not optional. "And there is salvation in no one else; for there is no other name under heaven that has been given among men by which we must be saved" (4:12). Jesus Himself declared, "I am the way, and the truth, and the life; no one comes to the Father but through Me" (John 14:6). The New Testament makes a claim of exclusivity in regard to Jesus. Either one chooses to obey the gospel and be saved from sin, or he chooses to reject the one and only plan of salvation. The result of rejecting Jesus as the Son of God and refusing the gospel is disastrous (John 3:16; 2 Thessalonians 1:8–9). Have you made this life-changing choice?

I.   Three Truths About Christianity.
    A.   Christianity is an historical faith. The claims of the Bible are not "once upon a time in a far away land," but are, instead,

rooted in historical events. How do you know, for example, that George Washington lived or that Abraham Lincoln was a real person? You never saw them and yet you can believe based upon evidence: (1) the testimony of those who saw them and wrote about it, and (2) artifacts from that era that corresponds favorably with the testimony. Faith in Jesus is based upon the same kind of evidence. Luke, for example, writes in the context of history giving us names, places, times, events—that can be verified and collaborated (Luke 1:1–4; 2:1–2; 3:1–2).

1.   Someone may ask, "Do you have evidence that gives you 100% certainty about Jesus?" No. I wasn't there and didn't see Him with my own eyes. But that's true with any historical event. Consider this:

When you get on an airplane, do you have 100% certainty that it won't crash? You can argue that based upon statistical evidence you have 99.9% certainty and, as a result, you board the plane. Yet how much of "you" climbs aboard? 100%!

When someone asks, "Do you have 100% proof that Jesus was real and that He died on the cross and was raised from the dead?" We reply negatively. "Then forget it," they say. Not so fast. Do you really want to close your eyes to the overwhelming evidence for the historical Jesus and the resurrection?

2.   Here is the question that must be asked: Is there enough evidence to warrant 100% commitment to Jesus Christ? *Yes!* The historical nature of Christianity must be based upon the same evidence used to judge any historical events. Given the eyewitness accounts (1 Peter 5:1; 2 Peter 1:16; 1 John 1:1–3), those willing to die for their testimony, the amazing conversion of Saul of Tarsus, and the collaboration of non-biblical literature and archeology, we concur with the writer John who said, I haven't told

you everything about Jesus, but I have given you enough so that you can make an intelligent and reasonable decision (John 20:30–31).

3. No person of history has impacted the world like Jesus.

B. Christianity is an objective faith. Subjective faith suggests that you can believe whatever you wish as long as you believe it. As a result, subjective faith places all the emphasis on the person doing the believing. That is the very opposite of Christianity. When it comes to the gospel of Christ, the emphasis is not in the one trusting as much as it is in the one trusted, nor in the one believing as much as it is in the One believed.

1. Mormons and Muslims have faith, but the "object" of their faith is wrong. For Christians, the "object" of our faith is everything. If Jesus Christ is not who He claimed to be, then we have no basis for faith. If He was not virgin born (Isaiah 7:14), the Son of God (John 3:16), dead on the cross (1 Corinthians 15:3), and resurrected on the first day (Luke 24:6), our faith is worthless (1 Corinthians 15:17).

2. But our faith is not worthless. Paul exclaims, "For I know whom I have believed" (2 Timothy 1:12). Paul's faith centered on a central object: Jesus! Likewise, our faith is not the *subjective:* I believe because it feels right for me—but the *objective:* I believe because the evidence in favor of the object is overwhelming.

C. Christianity is an open faith—it remains open to examination and scrutiny. The apostles threw the resurrection on the table and challenged people to examine the evidence (1 Corinthians 15:4–8). Prophecy is certainly open to examination (how do you explain over 300 prophecies about the Messiah finding fulfillment in Jesus?). What evidence does the unbeliever have that would discredit my faith? The evidence weighs heavy in favor of the believer—not the unbeliever.

*The skeptic announces, "Christianity is a leap into the dark!"
Hardly. The truth is, Christianity is a leap into the light! The
person running around in the dark is the one without evidence.
When it comes to evidences for the reliability of Jesus and the
gospel, the evidence is overwhelming.*

II. Acts 16:30—"Sirs, What Must I Do to be Saved?"
*Is there a greater question that can ever be asked? Note the five
implications within the question itself:*

   A. The question.

      1. What must I do to be *saved?* The word "saved" implies that
I am lost.

      2. What must I *do* to be saved? The word "do" implies action
on my part.

      3. What must *"I"* do to be saved? The word "I" implies
personal responsibility—no one can do this for me.

      4. What *must* I do to be saved? The word "must" implies
conviction, necessity, and immediacy.

      5. *What* must I do to be saved? The word "what" implies a
search for answers outside of self.

   B. The answer—"Believe in the Lord Jesus, and you will be
saved" (v. 31). Paul isn't suggesting the kind of shallow faith
often promoted today—a mere mental acknowledgement
that Jesus is the Christ. Paul speaks of intelligent conviction
based upon evidence (Romans 10:17). In all probability, this
Gentile jailer knew nothing about Jesus. As a result, Paul
"spoke the word of the Lord to him" (v. 32). The "word of the
Lord" was inclusive of what he needed to do to respond to
the Lord. It's no surprise what happened next. Note the
immediacy (v. 33). The jailer learned (1) what God did to
procure his salvation and (2) what he must do to receive it. As
a result, there was much rejoicing (v. 34). He heard, he
believed, and he obeyed.

   C. Grace is God's part; faith is our part. But what kind of faith
saves? Saving faith is faith that obeys God's commands.

1. Saving faith leads to repentance, Acts 2:38. Repentance involves a change of will regarding sin. It is prompted by godly sorrow over your past (2 Corinthians 7:10) and results in a change of direction (Acts 3:19). Hence the question: is your faith strong enough to change your behavior?

2. Saving faith leads to confession, 1 Timothy 6:12–13. Someone asks, "Is a public confession necessary?" A confession is not a confession unless it is articulated in some public form (Matthew 10:32; Acts 8:37). A confession merely announces to others that you are changing allegiance and serving a new Master.

3. Saving faith leads to baptism for the remission of sins, Acts 22:16; 1 Corinthians 12:13; Galatians 3:27; Romans 6:3. Baptism is the final action of faith that brings one into Jesus Christ and the blessings of the gospel.

Discussion Questions
Prompting Additional Insight

1. How would you respond to the following objections that are often used to justify one's refusal to obey the gospel?
   —I believe salvation is by grace...
   —I'm just not good enough. If you knew all I've done...
   —There are too many Christians who are hypocrites...
   —I don't know enough...
   —I am almost persuaded...

2. What sets Jesus apart from every other religious leader?

3. What are the consequences of rejecting the gospel (2 Thessalonians 1:8–9)?

4. Baptism is often the "hang up" in the minds of many as they have been taught "salvation by faith only." And although they expand

"faith only" to include the actions of repentance and confession, they stop short when it comes to baptism. Consider/discuss this illustration:

When we lived in Texas and traveled back to Tennessee, we crossed the Mississippi River at Memphis. To go from the state of Arkansas to the state of Tennessee we had to cross the bridge and take the last step. One step took us from one state and deposited us into another.

When it comes to the gospel, we aren't talking about geographical boundaries, but relationships. Baptism is the final action of faith that puts one "into" Christ (Romans 6:3). As long as one maintains "faith only," their spiritual state remains unchanged. For example, I could stand in West Memphis, Arkansas and believe with all my heart that I was in Tennessee, but it didn't make it so. To be in Tennessee, I had to take the final step that placed me there. To be in Christ, I had to take the final step that placed me in a right relationship with Him. All of which means that if you have never been baptized for the remission of sins, you remain in a foreign state, alienated from God's blessings. It doesn't have to be. "Arise and be baptized and wash away your sins" (Acts 22:16). It will be the most life-changing choice you will ever make.

I Choose to Grow as a Child of God

Colossians 3:1–17

Therefore if you have been raised up with Christ,
keep seeking the things above...

News stories of irresponsible parents who neglect their children find no sympathy with right-thinking people. In fact, those stories enrage us. How could they neglect them? How could they abandon their precious children to fend for themselves?

Then, again, how can we?

New Christians are called "newborn babes" (1 Peter 2:2). Paul describes those young in the faith as "infants in Christ" (1 Corinthians 3:1). Do we leave a spiritual newborn alone to "fend for himself?" Hardly. Young Christians need to learn the basics of what God expects from them and they also need the encouragement of older saints who serve as a source of strength and friendship.

Sometimes we don't think through the changes God expects when one becomes a Christian. The fact is, the Lord demands that we be committed to re-tooling our entire life-focus. Obviously we must teach, support, and mentor them to do that. At the same time, they must also take personal responsibility and possess a desire to grow and learn. Sadly, too many new Christians see the action of obeying the gospel as the final step to salvation. It isn't. In reality, it is the first step toward a lifetime of growing up in Christ (2 Peter 3:18).

I'm a new Christian—now what?

I.   You Have a New Life—But what does that mean?

   A.   It means you are living under a new authority, v. 1. Paul declares the very first thing a new Christian must do is recognize the rank and rule of Jesus. His position at the right hand of God signifies His authority. A Christian, therefore, lovingly submits to his new Master and Lord. Thus, the overriding question in everything considered is: What does the Lord want me to do? What decision would please Him? What attitude should I manifest?

   B.   It means you are driven by a new hope, v. 2. Our motivation centers on the hope of heaven. As a result, we are heaven-driven and not earth-driven (Matthew 6:19–21). When our attention and affection shifts from the things below to the things above, it changes our perspective on everything.

   C.   It means you invite a new example, vv. 3–4. "Your life is hidden in Christ" means that He becomes your *everything*. Perhaps it is captured best by the lyrics of an American folk hymn—

He is my everything, He is my all.
He is my everything, both great and small.

Romans 8:29 tells us that we are to be "conformed to the image of His Son." Our life has taken a new turn. Those who know us best begin to see someone different. "You've changed!" they say. In fact, they are "surprised" when we no longer spend time with the worldly crowd (1 Peter 4:4).

II. You Must Kill the Old Man of Sin, v. 5.

The word translated "dead" means to slay or to mortify. Living for Christ means that certain attitudes and behaviors must stop. It's as if Jesus draws a line in the sand and says, "No more!" You have died to those things (see also Romans 6:1–7). *Note:* twelve attitudes and actions that must cease.

1. *Sexual immorality,* v. 5. This would include every relationship outside the boundaries of God-approved marriage. While God made us sexual beings, He limits our sexual expression to that special (and sacred!) relationship (Hebrews 13:4). In other words, a Christian cannot live sexually like the world. And that is very hard for some. Yet death is always hard. God is plain: Kill immorality!

2. *Impurity.* This is sexuality taken to the next level and describes one driven by fleshly lusts. Christianity involves more than "you can look, but not touch"; Christianity challenges us to stop looking (Matthew 5:27–28). We must work to discipline our mind with purity (Philippians 4:8).

3. *Passion.* It is sometimes rendered "inordinate affection" (KJV) and may refer to unnatural affection or homosexuality (Romans 1:26–27). And regardless of society, the Christian learns to be repulsed by what repulses God.

4. *Evil desire.* This involves anything God forbids. Some like to dabble in wickedness and enjoy the thrill of seeing how close they can get to the line without crossing over. God says, If you are going to follow Me, put to death that tendency.

5. *Greed.* This is covetousness "which amounts to idolatry." Here is one fixated on money, things, power, or a relationship he cannot have. The message: Kill it! Note: The reminder of coming judgment serves as great motivation (v. 6) although this is not going to be easy as old habits are hard to break (v. 7).

6. *Anger,* v. 8. Here is one who "loses his temper." How easy it is to excuse such outbursts with—"That's just the way I am." Not if you're a Christian! That behavior must end.

7. *Wrath.* Here is anger that escalates.

8. *Malice.* Anger taken to this level allows hatred to invade the heart. There is a desire to get even and even injure another.

9. *Slander.* It could be translated "vengeance" and a desire to hurt someone with words.

10. *Abusive speech.* This is obscene talk. Foul language is exactly that—it's out of bounds. The Christian must clean up his speech.

11. *Lying,* v. 9. Deception may be a habit of your past and a continued habit of the world, but God's people speak the truth (v.10).

12. *Racial prejudice,* v. 11. Racial bigotry was alive and well then as now. If "Christ is all, and in all" then all men are one in Him.

III. You Must Put on the New Man of Righteousness.

Being a Christian involves more than stopping certain behavior. There is a positive turn. Using Paul's analogy of a change in garments, we "take off" in order to "put on." Like the toddler who has been from the pool to the sandbox and then seeks entrance into the house only to be met by Mom who says, "Hold it! Take those off and put these on." So God expects us to put off the old behavior and put on the new. *Note:* twelve attitudes and actions that must be adopted.

1. *A heart of compassion,* v. 12. If Jesus cares about others, so must we (Galatians 6:10; Romans 12:15). One mark of Christian growth is when we step out of our selfish shadow and reach out.

2. *Kindness.* If anything has gone AWOL in our culture it is simple gestures of kindness and courtesy.

3. *Humility.* James reminds us that "God is opposed to the proud" (4:6) while Paul exhorts us to "do nothing from selfishness or empty conceit, but with humility of mind regard one another as more important than yourselves." Humility must also be our hallmark when it comes to open reception to God's instruction (James 1:21).

4. *Gentleness.* This speaks of harnessing strength and originally referred to the taming of an animal. It bespeaks a life of discipline and control.

5. *Patience.* One of the hardest of all life-lessons is learning to wait with patience (Isaiah 40:31).

6. *Bearing with one another,* v. 13. The key to unity in God's family is working hard to get along in spite of personality differences.

7. *Forgiving each other.* Paul puts our forgiveness of others into perspective—"just as the Lord forgave you, so also should you."

What we forgive others is small in comparison.

8. *Love*, v. 14. Love is the bond that holds everything together.

9. *The peace of Christ must rule*, v. 15. Worry about nothing and pray about everything is the prerequisite to peace (Philippians 4:6–7).

10. *Thankfulness.* Rather than complaining because everything isn't perfect, be grateful for what you have.

11. *Let the word of Christ richly dwell in you*, v. 16. How? Read it! Live it! Make it a part of your daily discipline.

12. *Be totally committed*, v. 17. *Note:* we are taken full circle back to where we began in verse 1.

Discussion Questions
Prompting Additional Insight

1. Discuss some of the reasons new Christians fall away—such as:
   —Family and/or relationship prejudices to Christianity
   —The pull of the world back to previous behavior patterns
   —A refusal to cut ties with "bad company"
   —Misunderstanding the depth of commitment to Christ
   —A lack of patience and/or attention by other Christians

2. Why is recognition of Jesus' authority (v. 1) the first and most crucial truth a new convert must grasp?

3. What does Paul mean when he says in verse 4, "Your life is hidden with Christ?"

4. According to verse 5, what must happen to the old man of sin?

5. What advice would you offer a new Christian about ways to overcome any of the problem areas mentioned in verses 5–11?

6. How would you respond to a Christian who excuses continued sinful behavior—whether it is impurity or temper or prejudice, etc.—with the excuse: "Well, that's just the way I am!"

7. Look at each of the twelve positive elements (vv. 12–17) that we are to add to our lives and discuss why each is crucial to our character.

8. An addiction counselor gave the following advice to anyone seeking to change their life from destructive behavioral patterns to those reflecting Christ. Putting it into simple terms, he said there are three essentials. "You must change your (1) playmates, (2) your play things, and (3) your playground." What do you think he meant?

9. Of Paul's list of twelve traits to "put on," name one or more that you need to work on.

I Choose to Forgive Others

Matthew 6:12, 14–15

*For if you forgive others for their transgressions, your heavenly Father
will also forgive you. But if you do not forgive others,
then your Father will not forgive your transgressions.*

When you make the choice to become a Christian and are
baptized for the forgiveness of your sins, you are then faced
with another choice. Now that you are forgiven, will you forgive
others who sin against you? It is one of the most powerful choices you
will ever make.

A failure to forgive others is like allowing toxic trash to fill up our
emotional suitcases—mental luggage that we lug around every
where we go. And those suitcases only get heavier with time.
Extending mercy, however, is a gift from God that frees us from the
weight of relational failure. Forgiveness disposes of hurts, betrayals,
disappointments, and whatever else we keep stuffing into our mental
attic. The best thing about forgiving others is that it sets us free.

While it is impossible to go back in time and do things differently, it
is possible to move forward a lot lighter. But only if we make this life-
changing choice: I choose to forgive.

There are some Bible verses difficult to understand.
Matthew 6:14–15 isn't one of them.

You forgive—*God forgives.*
You don't—*He won't.*

It's as simple as that.

I. No Choices Are Harder to Make Than This One.

    A. Forgiveness is an act of the will. Emotionally we seek to get back or get even with one who has hurt us. Forgiveness, on the other hand, involves a deliberate decision of the will to release another from the debt they have incurred. When someone has hurt us, stolen from us, lied about us, etc., we put them in a cage. Forgiveness opens the cage and cancels the debt.

    B. Some debts are more easily canceled. When loses are tangible, forgiveness comes easier. *You took my parking space. You borrowed my shovel and didn't bring it back. You accepted a $100 loan when you were in need and conveniently forgot about it.* In the grand scheme of things, none of those loses are a big deal.

        1. But what about intangible loses? *You took my dignity. You stole my purity. You destroyed my dreams for a happy marriage.* Now we're talking about some complex stuff because what was taken cannot be seen or returned.

        2. It is important to grasp that forgiveness does not minimize the pain, but *maximizes* your confidence in God to enable you to move forward without the weight of bitterness. It is exactly the emotional freedom captured by the words of Joseph in the aftermath of his relational pain: "God has made me forget all my trouble," (Genesis 41:51). God is the only One with the power to do that.

    C. What other choice do you have? You cannot change the past. You can choose to keep carrying the hurt forward. You can choose to nurse your wounds. You can keep lugging that luggage of bitterness, but the weight will only get heavier and eventually will do a number on you. Failing to forgive is cancer of the soul. It eats away slowly. And the person it consumes is *you!*

        1. Apparently some Christians think they can experience God's forgiveness yet withhold the same from others. It will not happen.

2. If you are unforgiving, no matter what you claim about knowing Jesus, Jesus says otherwise (Matthew 6:14–15).

Clearing Up Some Confusion

1. **Forgiveness doesn't mean you totally forget their sin.** That is unrealistic and impossible. The human mind captures scenes and stores them. Joseph never literally forgot what his brothers did. He did, however, allow God to bring him to a place where their sin didn't hurt him any more. And He will do the same for you. While you recall it, you make the choice not to dwell on it any longer.

2. **Forgiveness doesn't mean you place yourself in a position to be injured again.** Jesus' teaching is not promoting naïveté nor is it to become an excuse to enable sinful behavior to continue. We all know those who have used forgiveness and grace as excuses to continue in sin—the very thing Paul said must not happen (Romans 6:1–2). As the injured one, you have every right to say—We're not going there again! Forgiveness does not remove the need for accountability nor should it be used to enable sin. There are consequences to behavior—and even God's forgiveness does not remove accountability or consequences.

Holding one accountable is quite different than harboring bitterness by refusing to let go of a wrong. *Please note:* you don't let it go and the wrong disappears into thin air. You let it go into the hands of God. You give your grief to Him and pray for His wisdom.

II. What About Luke 17:3?

    A. Some argue that you are only required to forgive if someone asks for it. Look closer at the passage. *Q:* If my brother repents, should I forgive him? *A:* Absolutely! But let's look at it another way. Do you really think Jesus is saying—But if your brother doesn't ask, you can hold a grudge, nurse the pain, and become bitter?

1. Luke 23:34—Did Jesus' enemies ask for forgiveness? No.
2. Acts 7:60—Did Stephen's enemies ask for forgiveness? No.
3. In each case, Jesus and Stephen released their enemies into the hands of God. Each forgave and turned the justice-mercy issue over to Him.

B. We must understand two things: (1) just because we release someone doesn't mean God does (Romans 12:19), and (2) just because we release someone doesn't mean we announce our forgiveness to him. What if the other person has no desire for reconciliation or refuses to admit the wrong? There is no need to announce something that isn't sought. Pray about it, leave it at the Throne, and release it. That's what Jesus did. And Stephen. And Joseph. Joseph released his brothers long before they ever asked for forgiveness or showed up in Egypt.

III. How Important is the Issue of Forgiveness? *Matthew 18:21–35.*

A. By the first century, Jewish leaders taught you must forgive someone three times (three strikes and you're out). Peter said, Lord, if Andrew were to sin against me, I would forgive him up to seven times! Peter took Jewish tradition, doubled it, and added one for good measure. He was all smiles as he waited for another "Blessed are you Simon" moment. It didn't happen. Instead Jesus replied, "I do not say to you, up to seven times, but up to seventy times seven" (v. 22).

1. Jesus' answer had nothing to do with numbers. After all, it was Peter, not Jesus, who had introduced numbers. Jesus' point was that forgiveness doesn't keep count (1 Corinthians 13:5). He proceeded to illustrate His point with a simple story (vv. 23–35).
2. The king in the story is God. The one owing the impossible debt is *you.* The one owing the payable debt is whoever

has sinned against you. The bigger story here is not what
someone owes you, but what you owe the king.

3. Holiness demanded an accounting—and the debt was *paid
in full*. Since you could not pay it, Jesus did (John 3:16).

B. This is exactly why you must let the Cross take hold of your
life—and change you. Christianity impacts us in many ways,
but one way is clear: it impacts us in the way we pass
along God's blessing of forgiveness to others. Only one who
has experienced forgiveness can do this. Have you made this
life-changing choice?

Discussion Questions
Prompting Additional Insight

1. How hard is it to forgive someone who has sinned against you?

2. Sometimes we think that because we don't drink, cheat on our
spouse, or use profanity anyway, that embracing Christ doesn't
require much change. Not so fast. What about issues such as
worry, bearing with one another, and forgiveness?

3. Discuss reasons (excuses) given as to why people refuse to
forgive:
—*The hurt is too big.* Is the size of the offense justification for
holding on to it?
—*Time will make it go away.* Like flat tires and dirty diapers, some
things don't fix themselves.
—*I'll forgive, but I won't forget.* Isn't that backward? How will you
ever forget (put it behind you) until you forgive? Forgiveness
means letting go so God can heal
—*I'll forgive when she says she's sorry.* What if she doesn't? Do
you really want to face God in judgment when He asks you about
your attitude toward _____ ? What did the Hebrew writer say he
expected from Christians in his day (6:9)?

—*I'll forgive, but someone has to make him pay.* According to 2 Thessalonians 1:6; Romans 12:19, who is that "someone?"

4. When Jesus asked, "Father, forgive them; for they do not know what they are doing" (Luke 23:34), did the Father forgive them? When?

5. Matthew 18:24—Do some research and find out how much money this man owed the king. Matthew 18:28—Do some research and find out how much money this man was owed by his neighbor. What is the point?

6. In what ways will nursing bitterness and holding grudges destroy you?

7. Failing to forgive is like scattering garbage all over your house. What does God see in your house (heart)?

I Choose to Trust God When I Don't Understand

Psalm 118:1–6; Hebrews 2:13

The Lord is for me; I will not fear.
I will put my trust in Him.

Some think that because they are a Christian, all the hurts and complications of life will now disappear. That's not reality. Likewise, they think that by accepting Christ, all their questions will now be answered. That's not reality either. As a result, it's not uncommon to find Christians whose expectations are unrealistic to the point that they soon become disillusioned, discouraged, and fall away. One thing is true: our faith will be tested (James 1:2–3).

God is real no matter how you feel. It is essential that you know that. It's easy to have faith when everything is going well—you have great friends and family, a well-paying job, and enjoy good health. It's easy to have faith when, surrounded by others of like mind, you lift your voice and find it joined immediately by a chorus of other believers singing praises to God. It's easy to have faith when you walk beside a quiet beach or sit on a mountain peak while the hymn "How Great Thou Art" floods the soul. Those times, however, may be exceptions rather than the rule.

My life isn't always happy—is yours? My voice more times than not is usually alone rather than joined immediately by other believers. My mountain top experiences, although real, are rare compared to nights in the valley. Thus, the questions:
- How do I worship God when I don't *feel* like it?
- How do I grow in faith when things happen that I don't understand?

- How do I maintain a relationship with God when He seems, at times, so far away?

Yes, your faith will be tested. It will be tested not because God needs to know its strength, but because you need to know. And keep in mind—each of us is a work in progress and none of us have reached the point of perfection when it comes to faith. Faith, after all, is designed to grow and increase in strength (2 Peter 3:18).

I. Relationship is Tested by Separation.
   A. "Absence makes the heart grow fonder." That's not always true. Sometimes absence makes the heart grow weaker when, through separation, we lose our sense of closeness.
      1. All of us have had friends move away. In spite of our assurances that we will remain close, connected, and that nothing will change; in reality it does. Separated by time and distance we gradually grow apart. It can be the same with God.
      2. When you make the decision to become a Christian, you feel especially close to Him. Yet as you live each day in the real world of temptation, discouraging influences, physical difficulties, and unanswered questions, you can lose that sense of closeness. Suddenly you feel as if God is a million miles away. Rest assured; you are not the only one to ever wrestle with that or ask the questions: Why does God seem distant when I need Him? Where is God when I hurt?

      Psalm 10:1; 22:1–2; 43:2; Job 23:8–9

      3. The truth is: God had not walked away from the psalmists any more than He has walked away from you. The promise of Scripture is plain in both testaments: Deuteronomy 31:6, 8; Hebrews 13:5. That doesn't mean, however, that

you won't have feelings of absence and separation. Like you, there were times the writers of the psalms felt disconnected from God. But know this: their feelings betrayed them. And so will yours.

Our emotions are a wonderful gift from God and useful in many ways. However, they can be like a roller coaster as we experience the ups and downs of life. God, however, is unchanging. That's why we must focus on what we know rather than what we feel.

II. When God Seems Distant.
   A. Sometimes we feel disconnected from God because we are disconnected from Him. After all, sin does separate man from God (Isaiah 59:1–2). If there is ongoing sin in your life, don't blame God for something you have done. You are one who walked away, not Him.
      1. The good news in the parable of the prodigal is not only that the boy came home, but that he had a home to which he could come. And for one reason: his father never moved. It's the same with us.
      2. Sometimes, however, our feelings of separation from God have nothing to do with sin. Walking through "the valley of the shadow of death" we can feel very much alone. Yet the psalmist reminds us that regardless of how we feel, we are not alone (23:4).
   B. Herein is a common mistake: we seek a subjective feeling more than we seek Him. If the feeling happens we conclude that "God is with me during this tragedy." But if the feeling doesn't happen, we conclude that God doesn't care or has abandoned me. When that happens we have allowed our emotions to overtake truth.
      1. Feelings and facts can be two different things. Sometimes there is harmony as we feel what we know. At other times we find ourselves in such depths of discouragement that we begin to question if God cares.

2. Here is a *fact* you must remember: God is always present in the life of His child. "I will never desert you." "Never" is a big word. God uses it because He means it.

C. There will be situations in life where your faith will be stretched and God (if you go only by feelings) is nowhere to be found. How do you praise and trust God when life falls apart and heaven is silent? As one person said, "How do I keep my eyes on Jesus when they are full of tears?" The answer: there are times we must walk by the facts when the feelings aren't there (like David and Job). But how?

III. There are Four Things You Must Do *(when life is hard and you are tempted to allow your emotions to overtake your faith).*

A. *Tell God exactly how you feel.* Job did (7:11). God is such a trusted friend that you can tell Him anything. In fact, there is nothing about you that He does not know or cannot handle— your anger, doubt, fear, grief, confusion, etc. God let the likes of David and Job say what was on their heart—and still loved them.

Parent-Child—Do you want your children to communicate to you *only* what they think you want to hear? Or do you want them to tell you what's on their heart? Only on the basis of open communication is trust developed and trust leads to better understanding.

B. *Focus on God's unchanging nature.* Regardless of your circumstances or how you feel, confess what you know is true about God. I know God is good, that He loves me, that He knows what I'm going through, and that He cares (1 Peter 5:7). While our emotions are often up and down, God's character does not change.

C. *Trust God to keep His promises,* Psalm 118:6; Isaiah 42:6; Romans 8:28. We all experience long days and longer nights. We each have our "moments" when our spiritual tank is running low. That's when we must rely on His promises rather than our feelings. Mark verses of hope in your Bible and keep them handy. Share your heart with others you trust and pray together. Life is hard and sometimes it gets even harder. That's when you must stand on His promises.

D. *Remember what God has already done for you.* If God never did another thing for any of us, He still deserves our best because of what He has already done (Isaiah 53:6; 2 Corinthians 5:21). To think that He loved us enough to ask Jesus to die in our place, is the most remarkable fact of all (John 3:16). The next time you are going through the valley of suffering, look to the cross. Jesus' death for you is a fact that you must never forget or allow any feeling to ever erase.

Discussion Questions *Prompting Additional Insight*

1. Why do some new Christians have unrealistic expectations regarding faith—thinking that everything will go their way and all their questions will be answered?

2. Are Christians immune from suffering? What advantages do we have?

3. "Never doubt in the dark what God has told you in the light." What do you think that means?

4. Discuss the following statement that was scratched into a wall in Germany during World War II by someone hiding from the Nazi's.
   —*I believe in the sun even when it is not shining.*
   —*I believe in love even when I am alone.*
   —*I believe in God even when He is silent.*

5. "I Know That My Redeemer Lives" is a popular and faith-declaring hymn. It's easy while singing it to conclude that the

author was enjoying a mountaintop spiritual experience. Well, Job was the original author (19:25) and he wasn't on top of a mountain at all, but in the lowest valley of life. How was he able to make such a declaration? And note this: he didn't say, "I feel my redeemer lives..." Discuss.

6. It's easy to throw personal qualifications on God's love. *If God loved me, He wouldn't have let my sister die... taken my husband from me... let my parents divorce... allow the accident to happen...* While the answer to the "Why" question is often unanswerable (from our perspective), what is wrong with the original assertion: "If God loved me?

7. Why is it important for you to tell God how you really feel (instead of telling Him what you think He wants to hear)?

8. Parents sometimes forego explanations and tell their children, "On this one, you have to trust me." Does God not have the right to do the same with His children? Discuss.

LIFE-CHANGING CHOICE #7

I Choose to Love My Spouse

Ephesians 5:25; Titus 2:4

Husbands, love your wives as Christ loved the church...
Encourage the young women to love their husbands...

Two questions face us immediately:

1. *Do we really understand the meaning of true love?* It is easy to
    define love in terms of "feelings"—in fact many do. Let's set
    the record straight: while genuine love may include feelings
    of physical attraction, it goes well beyond that. A one-word
    definition of love is not feelings, but commitment. Ask couples
    married 20, 30, 40, 50+ years what is the secret to their marital
    longevity and my guess is that it's not goose-bump infatuation.
    What has made their marriage work is commitment. It is a
    commitment that for better or worse they would stay together,
    keep their promises, and work it out. And somewhere in their
    pursuit of unselfishness, they grew to love one another even more
    as the years came and went.

2. *Do we really understand how our marriage affects our message?* Is
    not the Christian's message one of forgiveness and reconciliation
    with God (1 Corinthians 5:17–19)? How does that square with two
    people who live in a home fraught with anger, animosity, distrust,
    and resentment? A marriage that is God-honoring puts flesh
    on the principle of reconciliation. Such a marriage will model
    forgiveness, sacrifice, and selfless love. And our children will
    know. And our brethren will know. And God will know.

A man fell in love with an opera singer. He was never close enough
to really know what she was like since his view was always from the
third balcony. She was obviously much older than he, but it didn't
matter. He fell in love with her voice and decided with a voice like

hers, he could live happily ever after. He set his mind on one thing—marriage.

After a whirlwind romance and a hurry-up ceremony, off they went on their honeymoon. It was then he watched in horror as she readied for bed. She pulled off her wig, ripped off her false eyelashes, yanked out her false teeth, plucked out her glass eye, unstrapped her wooden leg, and removed her hearing aids!

In shock and dismay he screamed, *"Sing woman, sing! Please, I beg you—sing!"*

> *Marriage is not as easy as it looks from the third balcony.*
> *It takes a lot of work and wisdom, prayer and patience.*

I. Wisdom from Proverbs: 24:3–4.

The riches Solomon describes cannot be bought. Equally so, they cannot be burned. Your house can be destroyed, but these riches will last. You cannot burn memories, relationships, character, and genuine love. The wise man is reminding us that our homes will not be strong because of what we have, but because of who we are. But it will cost: "wisdom," "understanding," and "knowledge." Wisdom is discernment from God. Understanding is responsive insight into the differences between the sexes. Knowledge involves a willingness to admit that maybe we don't know everything.

The bottom line of biblical counsel: "Unless the Lord builds the house, they labor in vain who build it" (Psalm 127:1).

II. Seven Musts for Love.
   A. Love is—leaving mom and dad and standing on your own four feet, Genesis 2:24. Some who marry shouldn't because either they aren't ready to cut the parental apron strings, or momma

and daddy won't let them go. It takes six people to make this principle work: the married couple plus two sets of parents.

1. If two people cannot live on their own physically, financially, and mentally, they have no business getting married. To abuse the first and most fundamental principle of marriage is to invite disaster from the beginning.

2. Husbands who marry a "daddy's girl" (fathers who have given them everything) will live with the constant frustration of being unable to provide the lifestyle to which she has been accustomed. Wives who marry a "momma's boy" will equally be frustrated in that she will never be free from a meddling mother-in-law.

3. Couples who violate this first and most basic principle will never find the happiness God seeks for them.

B. Love is—embracing the principle of permanence, Genesis 2:24. Two people pledge before God and man that they will remain together "until death do we part." Do those words mean anything? According to Jesus they do (Matthew 19:6). Commitment in a marriage means that each understands the permanency of this relationship. God's plan is clear: one man and one woman for life (Romans 7:2). And the one exception Jesus gives is exactly that—an exception (Matthew 19:9). Even then, through repentance, patience, and prayer, there can be reconciliation if both parties will cooperate with God.

C. Love is—coming together as one in unselfish acceptance, Genesis 2:24. While the "one flesh" speaks of the sexual union in marriage, it speaks to more than that. Two people from different backgrounds and with different temperaments, habits, scars, and interests are not going to automatically leave a ceremony and become "one" in the totality of all that God intends. The fact is: this involves a lifetime of growing up and old together (Ephesians 5:28–29). Decades may pass before the reality and totality of this kind of love becomes fully evident. But when it's there, you will know. Few things are more beautiful than to see an older couple in the sunset years of life who have genuinely become "one flesh."

D. Love is—the delight of sexual intimacy, Genesis 2:25; Song of Solomon; 1 Corinthians 7:2–5. God intends for there to be sexual intimacy in this relationship. Outside of marriage, it is dirty and defiled. Inside this union, it is a wonderful expression of love, beauty, and purity (Hebrews 13:4).

E. Love is—best friend communication, 1 Peter 3:7. How much time do you and your spouse set aside each week to engage in quiet time together? It may be as simple as half an hour over coffee after the kids are asleep or as planned as a morning breakfast together or an early evening walk around the neighborhood. In our modern era of immediate technology-connection with the outside world: the Internet, I-phones, texting, Facebook, etc., it's amazing how we can spend more time "connecting" with everyone else and less time connecting face-to-face with the one person who should be our best friend.

   1. "Live with your wife" literally means to dwell down and speaks of close companionship. And there can be no companionship without communication.

   2. Wives: make inquires of his world and gently bring him into yours. Husbands: step out of your world and learn to listen. The art of communication is fine-tuned by listening. Most of the time she doesn't want you to "fix" her problem as much as to "hear" what she says.

F. Love is—honoring her as the most important person in your life, 1 Peter 3:7. Most marriages don't fail over big things but over an accumulation of little things as each begins to take the other for granted. Work very hard to keep that from happening.

   1. Do you compliment your husband? Husbands appreciate hearing a simple "Thank You" for keeping the yard mowed, the car repaired, and the daily grind he faces in

the work world in order to support the family. And do more than the passing "Thanks!" as you walk out the door. Get his attention and tell him how much his providing and protection means to you.

2. Do you compliment your wife? Wives appreciate being told they look beautiful, that you notice the way they keep the house clean and well-appointed, and that you are thankful for their daily grind of mothering. A simple card or bouquet of fresh flowers from the grocery store means a lot.

G. Love is responding in loving submission to his headship, 1 Peter 3:5–6. When husbands lead in the spirit of Christ, most wives gladly respond. Leadership in the home isn't demanded; it's earned. Wives must ask the question: Do I respect my husband enough to allow him to take the reins of leadership in my home?

Discussion Questions
Prompting Additional Insight

1. Someone said, "Your marriage will either be a stumbling block or a stepping stone for the gospel message." Think: How does love for your spouse affect your presentation of the gospel to others?

2. Young people tend to see love in terms of physical attraction and infatuation. While not arguing against "chemistry," there is more to it than that. Allow discussion from those married 30 years+ as to what they have learned about the meaning of genuine love.

3. "For better or worse, for richer or poorer, in sickness and health, until death do we part." How serious is that vow and what does it mean?

4. *Men are from Mars, Women are from Venus* is the title of a popular book on the differences between male and female. God made us

"male and female" and besides the obvious physical differences, discuss our emotional differences and how each gender brings something very special and positive to the marriage relationship.

5. Discuss what "leave father and mother" means and doesn't mean.

6. Jesus allows one exception for divorce and remarriage (Matthew 19:9). But is the exception a necessity? Discuss some realistic and practical ways a couple can overcome this threatening sin and make their relationship stronger than ever.

7. How important is communication to a marriage? And how can each spouse work to make it better?

8. Think about how you treated your spouse this past week. Is that how you want your son or daughter to be treated by their spouse? Christianity involves more than believing certain truths as they relate to the local church and its work and worship. Christianity leaves the first day assembly and goes home with us. And no relationship tests more radically our love for God than in the way we treat our spouse. What are your thoughts?

I Choose to Raise My Kids to Serve the Lord

Joshua 24:15

...but as for me and my house, we will serve the Lord.

I t's not easy being a parent these days. The fact is: given the immoral climate of the 21st century, it is becoming increasingly difficult to raise up a godly family. With homosexuality moving culturally from toleration to acceptance and toward approval, to unrestrained profanity and immodesty (exhibitionism); from young people who show no respect for parents to parents who no longer demand it (because they are more interested in being their child's "best friend")—we have fallen into a sad sewer of sin (Proverbs 14:34). And our families are drowning.

We can become so accustomed to the rank and rottenness that we no longer recognize the stench (Jeremiah 6:15; 8:12). Sadly, those families taking a proactive stand for what is right, who monitor their children's behavior while demanding accountability and respect, are very much in the minority. Consider these two verses from Judges:

- *"And there arose another generation ... who did not know the Lord"* (2:10).
- *"In those days ... every man did what was right in his own eyes"* (17:6).

The second verse is a commentary on the first. If it could happen then, it can happen now. And it is happening now.

It has never been done. In the entire history of the NFL, no team has ever won three Super Bowls in a row. Only two teams in baseball have ever accomplished the feat (New York Yankees and Oakland

Athletics). In the NBA, only three teams: the Lakers, Bulls, and Celtics have pulled it off.

It is said to be the toughest challenge in all of sports. While it is incredibly hard to win one championship (much less two in a row), think of the obstacles of winning three: back-to-back-to-back. Sports writers have a one-word designation for the few who have pulled it off: "Dynasty."

Three-peating in sports is not nearly as tough as committing to the three-peat challenge of Moses in Deuteronomy 6 where God calls for back to back to back spiritual faithfulness in families.

I. God's 100 Year Challenge (Deuteronomy 6).
    A. It's tough enough to stand for God yourself (generation one). It's even tougher to raise up your kids for Christ (generation two). Toughest of all, however, is to raise up kids for Christ who will, in turn, raise up their kids for Christ (generation three). Here are three generations (approximately one hundred years) of faithful devotion to God. Yet it was exactly what God asked the parents in Moses' day to do. Does He expect any less from us?
    B. You may be thinking, "I don't have any grandchildren." Neither did most of them. Since the older generation perished in the wilderness (Numbers 14:29), the oldest people to whom Moses spoke were 59 years of age. Thus the vast majority of Israelites would have been younger families. Moses: I want you to think about your influence now and how it will affect generations that are yet unborn.
        1. You are probably thinking the same thing they were thinking. Wait a minute! I won't have a family one hundred years from now. But you're wrong. You will have a family then—you just won't be around to know them. But if you have raised your family to serve God, they will know about you.

2. All of which means—What you do today may impact how your family lives one hundred years from now. "So that you and your son and your grandson might fear the Lord."

II. The Question Is—How?

    A. First, grow your own faith, Deuteronomy 6:4–6. Take a highlighter and mark the words "you" or "your" in these verses. Before Moses ever says a word about "teaching them diligently" (v. 7), he emphasizes the need for you to be what God expects you to be.

        1. Moses: If you are trying to teach your kids about God without loving God yourself and putting Him first, forget it! Every home is either God-centered or self-centered— and your kids are quick to figure it out. And while you can preach to them until you run out of words, your walk will over shadow your talk.

Although kids are resilient, there is one thing they cannot handle: hypocrisy. And they can spot it a mile away.

        2. All of which means: parents must be people of the Book. Dads, read and know your Bible (Psalm 119:11; 2 Timothy 3:16–17). Moms, set an example of godliness in front of your kids (Proverbs 31:25–31; Titus 2:3–5).

        3. Yet, you can't have it in your heart if you don't know it. And if you don't know it, you can't pass it on to the next generation. "Fathers...bring them [your children] up in the discipline and instruction of the Lord" (Ephesians 6:4). Each parent must be proactive in the process.

           • Do your kids hear you talk about putting God first only to see you miss the Lord's Day assembly to pursue a hobby or watch a ball game? *What message has been sent?*

           • Do you tell your kids "not to talk down to others" only to have them hear you gossip and run down other

Christians? *What message has been sent?*

- Do you tell them not to use profanity or steal? Do you stress the importance of moral purity? What happens when they hear you curse, see you "borrow" what doesn't belong to you, or see you gawking at women? *What message has been sent?*

B. Second, Start today! Verse 7—
    And you shall teach them diligently to your sons
    and shall talk of them when you sit in your house
    and when you walk by the way
    and when you lie down and when you rise up.

1. How may I affect my family for the next one hundred years? By starting now. Not tomorrow, but NOW! It means I begin to walk obedient to God—today. It means I get back to reading the Bible—today. It means I start reinforcing God to my kids—today. It means I return to seriousness about my spiritual devotion and faith—today.

2. Since Paul zeroed in on fathers in Ephesians 6:4, let's do the same. If your child asks you a Bible question, don't shrug your shoulder and say, *I don't know: Go ask your mom—she's more into that.* Hear me clearly: Your child needs to see that you are into that. They need to see that you look forward to going to Bible class and the assembly. They need to see you participating in public worship and they need to see you up front serving the congregation. Is that what they see?

3. Each day provides new opportunities for you to "teach them diligently" (structured learning) as well as "talk of them" (informal learning or spur-of-the-moment opportunities). Be ready to take advantage of those times. Communicate openly. Turn off the TV (or any other distraction) and sit down as a family to eat (and talk) together. And make it natural and not forced.

C. Third, Pray! If you want to do something powerful for your family, become an Elijah-man of prayer (James 5:16–18). By the way, if you need direction and wisdom in order to parent more effectively, why don't you pray to the Father who knows how to be a father? James 4:2—"You do not have because you do not ask." Start asking!

Your job as a parent is not to be rich and famous, but to faithful yourself and raise your children to serve God. And then live to see your kids raise their kids to do the same. That, my friend, is a legacy that will live (forever).

Discussion Questions
Prompting Additional Insight

1. Deuteronomy 6 does not deny free moral agency or individual accountability (any more than Proverbs 22:6). Both passages communicate a truism that if you do your job as a parent, the odds go up dramatically that your children will also serve God (remember the saying, Like father, like son). Discuss two dangers: (1) concluding that every prodigal child is the fault of the parents, and (2) deciding that because you are a Christian your child will automatically become one, too.

2. Calculate the year 100 years from now. Where will you be? Where will your grandchildren be? Where will your great-grandchildren be? Why is that important to think about now?

3. The age of accountability—When it comes to young children who may wish to become Christians before they are old enough, how do we encourage without discouraging?

4. Every family tree has some strong spiritual branches and some weak ones. Discuss a family member of the past who made a positive impact on your life and walk with God.

5. Ephesians 6:4—Why do you think Paul singled out fathers?

6. Why is it important for our children to see parents involved in kingdom work—teaching Bible classes, leading prayer, waiting on the Lord's Table, showing hospitality to other Christians, cleaning the church building, etc.?

7. Why do some parents focus more on being their child's best friend than being a responsible parent? And why does there seem to be an abundance of passive parenting? And whatever happened to biblical discipline?

8. Someone noted that at the end of life, no one ever says, "I wish I had spent more time at the office." What's the point?

9. Why is this life-changing choice so important?

LIFE-CHANGING CHOICE #9

I Choose to Serve
Matthew 20:26–28

...whoever wishes to become great among you shall be your servant,
and whoever wishes to be first among you shall be your slave:
just as the Son of Man did not come to be served,
but to serve, and to give His life a ransom for many.

You are destined for greatness! While that sounds like the latest book release from the proponents of the health and wealth gospel, it is, in fact, 100% true! God wants you to grasp the true meaning of life by grasping the true meaning of greatness. There is, however, one catch: you must allow *Him* to define "greatness." Please be advised that His definition runs counterintuitive to the strategy of most.

God wants you to become great by becoming a servant.

You're kidding, right? No. God wants you to conform to the image of His Son (Rom.8:29)—and that image is one of serving (Mark 10:45).

I don't know if you've noticed but there aren't many servants around these days. After all, we live in a culture that is quite impersonal and self-serving. Not only do neighbors no longer visit across the backyard fence, they can't even see over it! We occupy common space but have very little contact with others. We send text messages by the hundreds but struggle with face-to-face encounters. It's like we're on a perpetual elevator ride where smiling, talking, and connecting are not allowed. Is the church immune? Hardly. Yet it is here—in the life-changing choice to serve—that genuine happiness is found and where God's people can make the biggest difference.

I. Servant or Celebrity? (Matthew 20:20–28)

 A. It's easy to be tough on Mrs. Zebedee. After all, she was proud of her sons and wanted them to succeed. She showed respect for Jesus and did not ask that her boys have His throne (only thrones #2 and #3). She certainly wasn't the first to think about greatness in terms of celebrity status.

  1. The other ten disciples were "indignant" (v. 24), but more for the fact that James and John beat them to the punch than anything praiseworthy on their part. All of them were competing for the top positions at the head table in the kingdom (Mark 9:33–35).

  2. "But Jesus answered, 'You do not know what you are asking'" (v. 22). She thought she did. Jesus is going to be the king in this new kingdom, right? Kings need rulers and rulers sit on thrones, right? After all, my boys are charter members, right? She was clueless. Jesus knew that one sip from His cup of suffering and her boys would flee into the night (26:56).

  3. Jesus used the opportunity to showcase the difference between the world's definition of greatness and His own (vv. 25–28). On any level of the public or private sector, it's all about being in charge. We watch in amazement as people play "politics" in order to climb the ladder and get the promotion. It happens every day and on any level.

 B. Jesus does not condemn James and John for seeking greatness as much as He works to help them redefine what it is. As always, Jesus found His "teachable moment" by emphasizing servant, not celebrity.

II. Greatness Is Not About—

 A. *Position.* It's easy to allow "position" to define us. From the company CEO to the professor at the university, from the politician running for the mayor's office to the preacher or elder in the local church, we zero-in on "position." The reason, however, that greatness does not equate with position is because position doesn't last. "Great today and gone tomorrow" sums up how quickly we can rise and fall in human terms. None of us are irreplaceable.

B. *Power*. Does the name "Barney Fife" ring a bell? Power can be intoxicating to some and a little authority can go a long way. Jesus said, "It is not this way among you" (v.26a). There are always obvious signs when people pack their bags for a power trip.

    1. Do we keep reminding others of who we are? "I am an elder of this church!" "I am the preacher!" "I am Dr. Jones with a PhD!" Someone said that if you have to tell people you're the boss (or wear the pants) you're obviously not. There may be a place for titles of respect in the world, but not among brethren in Christ's kingdom.

    2. Do we demand privileges? Few "crimes" are as bad as parking your car in my usual space nearest the church building (unless it's parking yourself in my usual church pew). When we expect special and/or preferential treatment, it's obvious that power has gone to our head.

    3. Do we feel threatened if we are questioned? Are we so full of ourselves as teachers that we think we "know" it all? Is it possible that we could be wrong? Is our name spelled D-I-O-T-R-E-P-H-E-S (3 John 9)?

C. *Praise*. Another tell-tale sign of a misunderstanding of greatness is when we begin to enjoy praise. While it's not wrong for people to recognize our talents, success, etc., it must pass from one ear to the other and not get stuck in between. Each must ask the question of 4:7 (1 Corinthians 4:7) followed by the admission of 4:7 (2 Corinthians 4:7). In other words, the glory belongs to God, not self.

III. Greatness is About Serving.

A. The Corinthians had "preacher-itis." Paul chastised them for such and exclaimed, "What then is Apollos? And what is Paul? Servants through whom you believed" (1 Corinthians

3:5). When Paul thought of himself, "servant" was the word
he used most (Romans 1:1; 1 Corinthians 3:5; 4:1; 9:19;
2 Corinthians 4:5; 6:4; 11:23; Galatians 1:10; Philippians 1:1;
Titus 1:1). When he wrote to Timothy about being a gospel
preacher, he reminded him to be a servant (1 Timothy 4:6;
2 Timothy 2:24). And when he recommended Christians by
name, he often did so by pointing out their servant-heart
(Romans 16:1, 6; Colossians 4:12).

B. Jesus asked, "Who is the greatest in the kingdom of heaven?"
According to Matthew 18:1–4, it isn't who you might think. In
fact, it is those who do not know they are. The greatest person
is the servant (Matthew 20:26).

1. Who is the greatest person in the local church? Again, it is
the one who serves! What a radical reversal of thinking
from what the world expects. And how do I serve? We are
admonished in Romans 12:6–8 to use our talents in our
particular area of giftedness.

2. Your life as a Christian means nothing until you learn to
serve.

- It's teaching a Bible class and helping others learn.
- It's visiting an elderly member at the nursing home.
- It's preparing the Lord's Supper.
- It's cleaning the building, locking up after everyone
leaves, and keeping the lawn mowed and trimmed.
- It's reaching out to a frazzled young mom.
- It's extending hospitality, writing a note of
encouragement, and offering a shoulder to one who is
hurting.

It is all of these and more! After Jesus washed the feet of
the Twelve, He said, "For I gave you an example that you
also should do as I did to you" (John 13:15). He didn't say
to assemble in a Bible class in order to analyze and
diagram what He did—He said, Do as I did to you.

C. The breakthrough in our Christian life occurs when we make
the life-changing choice to serve others. Serving is not

something for which you wait to be asked. Be proactive! This business of *"Call me if you need anything"* is often meaningless. There is always a need. Volunteer!

D. Jesus sets the standard so high that the only way to reach it is to look low. And He should know. The King of kings and Prince of the world was introduced on a bed of straw in a smelly stable. And once He was grown, He didn't change. He wasn't afraid to rub shoulders with the sick, put His arm around the hurting, and wash the feet of those who thought they were too good for menial tasks. And what does He ask from His followers? The same. If you want a serious upgrade on your life, become a humble servant. You will never be happier.

Discussion Questions
Prompting Additional Insight

1. A class in medical school was given a pop quiz. The test was relatively simple until the last question. "What is the name of the woman who cleans this building?" The students thought the question was a joke. One young lady handed in her paper and asked if the last question would count toward her grade. "Absolutely," said the professor. He went on to say, "In your career you will meet many people and each is significant. Every person on any level deserves your attention and care even if all you do is learn their name and say 'Hello.'" The young lady later wrote, "I never forgot that lesson. I also learned that her name was Dorothy." How does this story relate to the local church?

2. How has your life been affected by the selfless service of others?

3. Think of someone in the congregation where you worship who has gone through difficult times. Mail them a handwritten note expressing appreciation for them and tell them you are lifting up in prayer.

4. Is Jesus telling us in Matthew 20:26 that we should never try to better ourselves? Personal ambition is something we should have (we see examples of those without any). However, how do we find the balance—keeping our feet on the ground while trying to reach for personal success?

5. What is your opinion of the mother of James and John?

6. A business man in first-class caught his flight and headed home. As he boarded the plane, he spotted a young soldier. Just before they departed, the businessman asked the flight attendant to bring the soldier up front. The man stuck out his hand, said "Thank You for serving our country," and then gave up his first-class seat for the solider. He refused to take no for an answer. The soldier told him it made his day. What he didn't know was that it made the other man's day, too. What is the principle of Acts 20:35?

7. What is the name of the cleaning lady (or man) in the building where you work?

I Choose to Stand

1 Corinthians 16:13; Galatians 5:1; Ephesians 6:11

Be on the alert, stand firm in the faith, act like men, be strong.
Therefore, keep standing firm . . . Put on the full armor of God, so that
you will be able to stand firm against the schemes of the devil.

Satan doesn't give up once you make the life-changing decision to become a Christian. If anything, he redoubles his effort to reclaim you for his "domain of darkness" (Colossians 1:13). Sadly, he is successful with many. Jesus described it in Luke 9:62 as putting the hand to the plow (making a decision to look ahead to Christ) and then looking back (feeling the pressure to return to the world). Peter painted a sickening word-picture of a "dog returning to its vomit and a sow returning to wallowing in the mire" (2 Peter 2:22).

It is in our post conversion weeks and months that reality sets in as we find ourselves surrounded by friends and families, coworkers and schoolmates, who may not comprehend or respect our faith. They may even delight in ridiculing our decision (1 Peter 4:4). Thus living for Jesus, making God-honoring decisions, and shinning our light in the midst of a darkened world can become extremely difficult for all Christians—young and old alike.

Knowing it would be tough, Jesus encourages us with these words: "Whoever confesses Me before men, I will also confess him before My Father who is in heaven" (Matthew 10:32). *If you will stand up for Me, I will recommend you on the Day of Judgment.*

So how do we find the courage to stand?

I. A Rooster Reminder—Matthew 26:31–35, 69–75

   A. Jesus prophesied what would happen. "You will all fall away because of Me this night" (v. 31). Peter was emboldened and declared that he would stand regardless of what the others did (v. 33). But Jesus knew better. "This very night, before a rooster crows, you will deny Me three times" (v. 34). It happened just like Jesus said it would (vv. 69–75).

      1. Let's be painfully real—we all have done the same thing. Each of us has had moments in which we could have stood but we froze instead. Have you heard the rooster crow?

         a. At work, when given the opportunity to speak on behalf of the One whose name is continually blasphemed and profaned, you remained silent.

         b. At school when peer pressure was exerted and you found it easier go along with the crowd than to take a stand.

         c. At family events that happen to coincide with your first day commitment to worship, you gave in because it wasn't worth the hassle.

      2. Christianity is more than sitting in a pew on Sunday. Christianity goes with us wherever we go and demands loyalty to Christ in every situation. Have you pledged your loyalty to Him? Are you still loyal or are you hearing the rooster crow?

   B. If you are going to be a follower of Jesus Christ, you must be willing to stand. You must be willing to fly the flag of your faith regardless of what others think. Living for Jesus means that you must have conviction, fidelity, grit, loyalty, and courage regardless. It is something about which you must be passionate and unashamed (Romans 1:16).

I cannot deny my Lord.
Every place I go. Every chance I get.
God, help me stand!

II. I Choose to *Stand* By—

A. *Spreading my salt,* Matthew 5:13. There is no denying the impact of salt. And there is no denying the impact of one person with the courage to stand up for the name of Christ. Yes, it's easier to go along to get along. Yes, it's easier to mind your own business. Yes, it's easier to keep your mouth shut. Salt, on the other hand, does one thing above all others: it makes an impact. Do others know you are a Christian? Do others know you stand for something? Are you making an impact?

1. Like Peter, we're afraid. I wonder sometimes if God doesn't shake His head at our passivity. Folks, we're Christians! We can't dress like the world, talk like the world, or frequent certain places of entertainment the world thinks little about. Our habits, priorities, and attitudes must be different. After all, our reputation is at stake. Beyond that, His reputation is at stake.

2. What happens to our salt when:

a. We go to Hooters or similar places where we are tempted to do the very thing Jesus said not to do (Matthew 5:28)?

b. We spend time at a public pool or water park where others appear in various stages of undress (1 Timothy 2:9)?

c. We watch TV shows or attend movies that glamorize adultery and homosexuality and where profanity is rampant (1 Thessalonians 4:7)?

d. We engage in social drinking in order to be accepted and appear sophisticated (1 Peter 4:3)?

3. There is an old saying, "If you don't stand for something you will fall for anything." Some of God's people are falling—and fast. Listen to the warning of Jesus: "but if the salt has become tasteless, how will it be made salty again? It is no longer good for anything." Salt that loses its potency is bland. What use is it then?

B. *Shining my light,* Matthew 5:14, 16. Jesus challenges us: Stop hiding your light! Jesus is not telling us to shine a spotlight in someone's eyes or to dump a truckload of salt. It usually doesn't take much to accomplish what is needed.

An Alabama teenager out with school friends had a decision to make. When the majority in the group decided to start drinking, he asked to be taken home. In the days following his decision to stand alone, his peers teased him unmercifully. A week later his life ended in a tragic auto accident. At the conclusion of the funeral, the same young people who had made life so hard for him made their way to the front and each dropped a card into the casket. Every card had essentially the same thing: *"I'm so sorry. Please forgive me."*

> Live for Jesus O my brother,
> His disciple ever be;
> Render not to any other,
> What alone the Lord's should be.
>
> Live for Jesus, Live for Jesus;
> Give Him all thou hast to give;
> On the cross the world's Redeemer,
> Gave His life that thou mightst live.
> —Eden Laitta, 1892

That young man made a decision to stand—
A decision he will never regret.

C. By surrendering my will to His, 1 Corinthians 16:13. Each of these twelve choices requires the same thing: a surrendered will. And until you surrender your will to His, you will be unable to live out any of them. In this verse we are challenged to (1) be watchful, (2) be determined, (3) be man-like in courage, and (4) be strong in our commitment.

D. By making the Scriptures my standard, 1 Thessalonians 2:13. Some things are non-negotiable. It is imperative as Christians that we take God at His word and follow that word by examining everything taught by the Scriptures (Acts 17:11).

1. After Paul's serious challenge to Timothy to "preach the

word" (2 Timothy 4:1–2), he gives the reason: "for the time will come when they will not endure sound doctrine; but wanting to have their ears tickled, they will accumulate for themselves teachers in accordance to their own desires " (vv. 3–4). Just as it is easy to go along with the worldly crowd when it comes to morality, it is equally easy to do the same with the religious crowd when it comes to God's plan for the worship and work of His church (1 Timothy 3:15).

2. The New Testament alone must be our guide and authority in everything we do. Sometimes standing against false teachers is the most difficult "standing" we are called to do (Matthew 7:15–16; 1 John 4:1). But it is a "stand" we must be willing to make.

Have you made the choice to stand for God regardless?

Discussion Questions
Prompting Additional Insight

1. Discuss the difficulties and advantages of standing up for Jesus in the following places:
   —1st century cities like Corinth, Thessalonica, Rome, etc.
   —21st century cities like your own
   —1950s rural America
   —In the Bible belt where God's people are plentiful
   —In regions where God's people are scarce

2. Give Biblical examples of those who had the courage to stand for righteousness when it wasn't easy to do so.

3. Why did Peter give in and lie about his association with Jesus?

4. Christianity is not intended to be a secret lifestyle. Yet the mindset of some seems to be—"Let's go to church on Sunday, but let's not get overly serious about this." As a result, they profess

"Christianity" on Sunday but live like the world every other day of the week. What does the Lord say about that mindset in Matthew 6:24; Revelation 3:15–16; and 1 John 2:15–17?

5. How does Paul tell us to live in Philippians 2:15?

6. What would you like to say to the mother of the deceased young man who made the choice to return home rather than remain with peers who began drinking?

7. How would you describe the difference between standing on your own strength and standing on the strength which God supplies?

8. What choice to stand is emphasized in Proverbs 23:23?

9. Taking a stand upon Scripture is not always popular—even in religious circles as we discuss the Bible with friends and neighbors. What are the implications of 1 Timothy 4:1–4 for us?

I Choose to Abound in Kingdom Work

1 Corinthians 15:58

*Therefore, my beloved brethren, be steadfast, immovable,
always abounding in the work of the Lord, knowing your toil
is not in vain in the Lord.*

D o you know any "couch potatoes?" A couch potato is defined as "an inactive person who lives a sedentary lifestyle." We usually think of someone who plops down in the recliner while holding a bag of chips in one hand and a diet cola in the other. Physicians stress regularly (and for good reason!) the importance of physical activity and exercise for the betterment of one's health.

Do you know any "pew potatoes?" A *pew potato* is someone who plops down weekly in a church pew (*their* pew!) while complaining often about critical matters such as—*The preacher went five minutes too long this morning! It was too hot (cold) in the building today! Sister _____ gives me a headache with her high-pitch singing! Speaking of singing, brother _____ can't carry a tune in a bucket!* The pew potato usually arrives late, leaves early, and complains because "no one in this church is friendly."

Pew potatoes are quite common.

Jesus was extremely blunt about those who think the totality of their involvement begins and ends with their name in a pictorial church directory. Addressing such tepid apathy at Laodicea, He said, "So because you are lukewarm, and neither hot nor cold, I will spit you out of my mouth" (Revelation 3:16). Half-hearted devotion is obviously no devotion at all.

I. God Expects Extra Effort from His People.

    A. When the apostle Paul ended his great dissertation on the resurrection, he challenged every believer in 1 Corinthians 15:58. *"Therefore, my beloved brethren"* (this challenge is for the Christian), *"be steadfast, immovable"* (this challenge requires loyalty and commitment), *"always abounding"* (this challenge involves extra effort), *"in the work of the Lord"* (this challenge involves an endeavor in a special cause— the Lord's cause), *"knowing your toil will not be in vain in the Lord"* (this challenge will be rewarded). Note:

       1. The Who? *"my beloved brethren"*

       2. The What? *"be steadfast, immovable"*

       3. The Where? *"in the work of the Lord"*

       4. The Why? *"knowing that your toil is not in vain"*

       5. The When? *"always abounding"*

    B. God expects His children to become a part of a local assembly of believers* (Hebrews 10:23–25) and to do so with the determination of active participation. The government may issue its "minimum standard requirement" regarding nutrition, but the force of Scripture knows nothing about *minimum* spiritual devotion.

       • Matthew 5:41—"If any ask you to go one mile, go with him *two.*"

       • 2 Corinthians 8:3—"*Beyond* their ability, they [Macedonians], gave of their own accord."

       • Galatians 6:10—"While we have opportunity, let us do good to all people, *especially* to those who are of the household of faith."

       • 1 Peter 3:15—"*Always* being ready to make a defense..."

       • 2 Peter 1:5—"Apply *all* diligence..."

       • Jude 3—"Contend *earnestly* for the faith..."

    *Each of the many "one another" commands of the New Testament are best fulfilled by association in a local assembly. Paul's letters to specific local churches plus his admonition to "obey your leaders and submit to them" (Hebrews 13:17) requires that we belong to a local church whereby we can grow, be accountable, and both give and receive encouragement. To argue in favor of being a "Christian at large" is to deny these necessary conclusions of Scripture.

C. God calls His people to go above and beyond. He requires more than the *NORM:* Non-inspired, Ordinary, Rote, and Mundane.

II. 212°—The Extra Degree.

Water boils at 212 degrees. And when water boils it makes steam. And steam harnessed can move a train! One degree makes all the difference.

A. It's amazing how seemingly small things matter. As Vince Lombardi said, "Inches make a champion." The secret between success at anything is no secret—it's extra effort. That's true in the business world, raising a God-fearing family, or being a part of a growing church. Success at anything is no accident.

1. It's not effort that is usually missing, but extra effort. If you don't believe that, ask the silver or bronze medal winners at the Olympics.

2. Or ask Paul. In fact, you don't have to because he spells it out in 2 Corinthians 11:23–28. His description of what he went through to work in the kingdom is jaw-dropping regardless of how many times you read it. Or ask Jesus Himself. He labored at times to the point of exhaustion (Mark 3:8–9, 20; 6:31).

B. What keeps us from giving extra effort?

1. *Preoccupation with hobbies and sports.* We get too many irons in the fire, involve our kids in limitless activities, and spend too much time focused on extra-curricular stuff. To my question, "What's your biggest frustration as a shepherd of God's people?"—one elder responded, "We have too many young families who don't make time for the Lord's work. It's even hard to find teachers willing to devote time to teaching Bible classes."

2. *Lost idealism.* Once reality sets in and we learn that most will reject the gospel, it's easy to stop trying altogether. Even though the sower is not always successful, he doesn't stop planting.

3. *Prosperity.* Does the church grow more in times of adversity or prosperity? Prosperous times are much like the feeling you get after eating a big meal—you would rather nap than work.

III. Our Problem is not Information, but Motivation.

A. The failure for most Christians and churches is not in knowing, but in doing. How easy it is to settle into the rut of status quo and decide to coast. Do you think the Lord is pleased with that?

1. To the church at Ephesus: "Repent and do the deeds you did at first."

2. To the church at Sardis: "Wake up, and strengthen the things that remain which were about to die."

3. To the church at Laodicea: "Be zealous and repent."

B. When it comes to kingdom work, there is work for everyone to do. Ephesians 4:16—"according to the working of each individual part." The physical body works only when every part works. It's the same with the local church.

1. Each of us needs to look at our spiritual commitment and ask: Am I giving effort or am I giving my *best* effort? Am I merely mediocre in my commitment or am I on *fire* for Christ? Am I coasting, or am I a "212" Christian?

2. It can be as simple as the decision we make to stay home on Wednesday night because we're not feeling 100% instead of pushing ourselves to come because someone needs our encouragement (and we need theirs). It can involve our dedication when it comes to giving financially—are we sacrificing or giving a token? And what about the use of our talents? Are we getting too comfortable pew-sitting or are we stepping out of our

shadow and participating and growing in ways that stretch us spiritually? Here it is for every local church:

- Elders—*extra* effort at shepherding
- Deacons—*extra* effort at serving
- Preachers—*extra* effort at teaching
- Bible class teachers—*extra* effort in the classroom
- Every Christian—*extra* effort when it comes to greeting guests, praying for one another, cleaning the building, waiting in hospital waiting rooms, taking food to the funeral home, leading the singing, and whatever else needs to be done.

Discussion Questions
Prompting Additional Insight

1. What does 1 Corinthians 15:58 mean to you?

2. Discuss the principle that the key to success in anything is extra effort.

3. One day a man was walking along the beach when he saw a boy picking something up and gently throwing it into the ocean. Approaching the boy, he asked, "What are you doing?" The youth replied, "I am throwing starfish back into the water. The surf is up and the tide is going out and if I don't throw them back, they will die." The man frowned and replied, "Son, don't you realize there are miles of beach and thousands of starfish? You can't possibly make a difference!" The boy listened respectfully as he bent down and threw yet another starfish back into the ocean. Then smiling at the man, he said, "I made a difference to that one!" What is the point of the story when it comes to the kingdom work of spreading the gospel?

4. A friend gets on a plane and flies to China to bring the gospel inside that Communist country. Not all of us have that

opportunity or are fitted to do what he does. In what ways can all of us "abound in kingdom work" (when it comes to foreign evangelism) for him and others who are willing to go?

5. Businesses motivate via a paycheck. Churches, on the other hand, motivate in the area of a payoff that will come later ("Your reward in heaven is great"). In other words, much of kingdom work is volunteer work. How can church leaders do a better job motivating volunteers to give the extra effort?

6. Discuss ways we can give extra effort when it comes to: (1) preparing for Sunday services, (2) singing, (3) giving, (4) greeting visitors, (5) advertising an upcoming gospel meeting, etc.

7. What would you tell an older saint who says there isn't much he/she can do anymore?

8. How excited are you about the Lord's work?

I Choose to Finish Strong, and Go to Heaven

In the January, 2011 issue of Biblical Insights *magazine, Sewell Hall and Dee Bowman wrote articles on the above topics. Although edited for space, they serve as a fitting conclusion to this study.*
Used by permission

I Choose to Finish Strong
By Sewell Hall

O f eight kings of Judah who are classified as good, six in their later years sinned and tarnished the reputation they had achieved in their early years. The same thing happens too often to faithful gospel preachers, diligent elders, effective teachers and godly women.

Causes of Failure

Some of the same things that caused the kings to sin in their later years may affect us as we grow older. After the death of a godly companion one may, like Solomon, marry someone who is a bad influence. Others, like Uzziah, may be dissatisfied with what they have achieved and become so ambitious for additional honors that they compromise their principles. Or, like Hezekiah, they may become so proud of what they have accomplished that they no longer feel dependent upon God for guidance and protection (2 Chronicles 32:25).

Love for the praise of men often leads to compromise. When significant errors first begin to be advanced among brethren, older men usually stand for the truth. But as increasing numbers accept the error, some yield to the pressure to conform. When a man has built a favorable reputation over a lifetime, it is difficult to take a position that will alienate him from his "fan club." Younger men who have no reputation to protect often find it easier to uphold an unpopular truth.

Then there is the problem of weariness that comes with age. Godly living is a fight (1 Timothy 6:12) and we may become tired of fighting. It is a race (Hebrews 12:1) and we may become tired of running. It involves "labor and suffering" (1 Timothy 4:10) and we may grow weary and feel that we have already done our part.

The idea in our culture is that after a person has put in a few years of productive labor he has the right to "retire and enjoy life." It is easy to let this notion affect our spiritual life. Jesus told of a farmer whose crop one year was large enough to make possible early retirement. He said to his soul, "Soul, you have many goods laid up for many years; take your ease, eat, drink, and be merry" (Luke 12:13–21). Our generation would commend him; Jesus called him a fool.

Perhaps less blameworthy is the feeling that we can no longer serve effectively and so we give up. It is important that we understand our limitations and not insist on continuing to serve in any capacity after age has limited our competence. But there are always other things we can do, sometimes with greater impact for good because of our age. The true servant of God will seek those new opportunities.

Advantages of Age

Retirement can actually increase opportunities to serve. Moses began his monumental work at the age of eighty. God did not let him retire. The experiences of those years were perfect preparation for his assignment. At retirement age, men who are still alert and healthy have more time to give to serving as elders and deacons. It is a pity if, instead of serving more effectively, they resign their responsibilities and go roving about the country pursuing their own pleasure.

Aging evangelists may not be as sharp and fluent as they once were, but they may find people listening more respectfully. Mothers when freed from the responsibilities of rearing children have more time to give to others (Luke 2:37).

Help for Finishing Strong
- *Prayer:* Psalm 78:17–18
- *Promises:* Isaiah 46:4
- *Exhortations:* Hebrews 10:36
- *Examples:* 2 Timothy 4:7–8

When the aged Polycarp was told that he could avoid the stake if he would deny his Lord, he replied, "Eighty-six years I have served Christ, and He never did me any wrong. How can I blaspheme my King who saved me?" Steadfast in his faith, Polycarp refused to compromise his faith and was burned at the stake.

Hebrews 12:1–2 serves as a fitting challenge for each of us to finish strong. As does Numbers 23:10—*Let me die the death of the righteous, and let my end be like his!*

I Choose to Go to Heaven
By Dee Bowman

Heaven: What is it?

The Bible avers heaven as the dwelling place of God, His eternal kingdom, as well as the dwelling place of His heavenly servants. When Jesus taught the disciples to pray, He began the prayer by "Our Father, which art in heaven" (Matthew 6:19). Is not God the height of heaven?" asked Job (22:12). David affirms the same in Ps.11:4: "The Lord is in His holy temple, the Lord's throne is in heaven." Furthermore, "the wrath of God is revealed from heaven against all ungodliness," warns Paul (Romans 1:18). God's power, control, and domination originate in Heaven.

Heaven is the original dwelling place of Jesus Christ. John 3:13 affirms that "no man hath ascended up to heaven, even the Son of Man which is in heaven." In John 6:68, Jesus said, "For I came down from heaven, not to do mine own will, but the will of Him that sent Me." Jesus returned there after having completed His work of redemption here on earth (Ephesians 4:10; 1 Peter 3:22). The Spirit's abode is likewise in heaven (John 14:26).

Heaven: *Where is it?*
I don't know.

Heaven: *Why is it?*
In addition to being the dwelling of the godhead, heaven is a place prepared for those who have been faithful during their sojourn on earth. David wrote in the Shepherd Psalm, "Surely goodness and mercy will follow me all the days of my life, and I will dwell in the house of the Lord forever (23:6). The beatitudes speak repeatedly of the heavenly home for the righteous. We are told by Jesus to "lay up treasures in heaven" (6:20).

Heaven is a place of reward for the saints—a reward so wonderful it is beyond our comprehension Peter speaks of the Lord's having given us "exceeding great and precious promises," so that we can have an entry way "into the everlasting kingdom of our Lord and Savior Jesus Christ (1:4, 11). Time and space prohibit the lavish description given of the heavenly abode in such passages as Revelation 7:9–17; 14:1–3; 21:1–11. There are not sufficient terms in our vocabulary to describe the joys and rewards of that heavenly abode, but God has given us a peek into its grandeur and beauty.

But being in the presence of God is the first and primary part of the reward for the faithful (John 14:3). Oh, the blessed thought of being with the Lord forever (1 Thessalonians 4:17). What joy! What bliss!

Imagine a place where God is the light, where there are no bad things of any sort, where sickness is never present, where tears of joy are the only ones, where we need never again contemplate sorrow or tolerate the heinous dealings of bad men, where we will have a peace never interrupted with any sort or kind of anxiety, where no phone ever rings with bad news, where friendship and love are not merely momentary, but eternal, where kindness and gratuity are not occasional or out of the ordinary, but a way of life, where the only labor is the kind we relish, so that we may offer uninterrupted praise to our Father, thanksgiving to His Son, adulation for revelation to His Spirit, where the sweet music of heaven is always in tune, where we join with angels to sing a blissful song of eternal praise, a song which comes easily out of spirits emboldened, even overwhelmed with love, adulation, and worship for the Holy One, the object of our now eternal affection.

Heaven: How Can I Get There?

And do you know what? It's a choice I can make. I can choose to go there. Now that's special. You mean the likes of me? One who is a sinner? Yes, sir. You can choose to follow Jesus (John 14:6) and become His disciple, by faith, repentance, confession, and baptism. Then live a faithful life and you can go there. It's your choice whether you go there or not. And remember this—

If you miss heaven, you've just missed all there is.

Discussion Questions
Prompting Additional Insight

1. Give reasons why some fail to finish strong.

2. Discuss the advantages and disadvantages of age when it comes to spiritual opportunities.

3. What is God's promise to the aging saint in Isaiah 46:4? What was Paul's reaction when he had the finish line in sight—2 Timothy 4:7–8?

4. What thoughts come to your mind when you consider heaven?

5. In addition to the scriptures that speak about heaven, one of the closest we come to gaining a glimpse of our reward is when we sing about it. Take a moment and peruse hymns about heaven and list two or three favorites.

6. What is Dee Bowman's conclusion about heaven and our choice?